AMERICAN COMMUNITIES

We Live in a SUBURB

Amy B. Rogers

press.

New York

Published in 2016 by The Rosen Publishing Group, Inc.
29 East 21st Street, New York, NY 10010

First Edition

Editor: Katie Kawa
Book Design: Reann Nye

Photo Credits: Cover, pp. 3–24 (background texture) Evgeny Karandaev/Shutterstock.com; cover Johnny Habell/Shutterstock.com; p. 5 Jenn Huls/Shutterstock.com; p. 6 Taras Vyshnya/Shutterstock.com; p. 9 Amy Tseng/Shutterstock.com; pp. 10, 24 (yard) Iriana Shiyan/Shutterstock.com; pp. 13, 24 (neighborhood) Konstantin L/Shutterstock.com; p. 14 Steve Nehf/Denver Post/Getty Images; p. 17 Ms.K/Shutterstock.com; pp. 18, 24 (bike) Monkey Business Images/Shutterstock.com; p. 21 Stuart Monk/Shutterstock.com; p. 22 karelnoppe/Shutterstock.com.

Cataloging-in-Publication Data

Rogers, Amy B.
We live in a suburb / by Amy B. Rogers.
p. cm. — (American communities)
Includes index.
ISBN 978-1-5081-4200-3 (pbk.)
ISBN 978-1-5081-4202-7 (6-pack)
ISBN 978-1-5081-4203-4 (library binding)
1. Suburbs — United States — Juvenile literature. 2. Suburban life — United States — Juvenile literature. I. Rogers, Amy B. II. Title.
HT352.U6 R58 2016
307.76'0973—d23

Manufactured in the United States of America

CPSIA Compliance Information: Batch #BW16PK: For Further Information contact Rosen Publishing, New York, New York at 1-800-237-9932

Contents

We like living in a suburb.
A suburb is also known as
a suburban community.

5

city

suburb

6

A suburb is an area outside a city or large town.

Many people who live in our suburb work in the city. They drive to the city every day to get to work.

9

10

There are many houses in our suburb. Each house has a big **yard** with a lot of grass.

Many of the homes in our suburb look alike. The homes are also close together.

13

We can see some wild animals near our homes.

We often see deer.
They eat the grass and other
plants near our homes.

17

18

We walk and ride **bikes** to get around our suburb.

Most kids in our suburb take the bus to school. Some kids walk to school.

21

We like to play together after school. We can play outside in our **neighborhood**.

Words to Know

 bike

 neighborhood

 yard

Index

B
bikes, 19
bus, 20

D
deer, 16

S
school, 20, 23

W
wild animals, 15

Y
yard, 11

Websites

Due to the changing nature of Internet links, PowerKids Press has developed an online list of websites related to the subject of this book. This site is updated regularly. Please use this link to access the list: www.powerkidslinks.com/acom/sub